THE SOUTHWEST

Excelsior House, Jefferson, Texas

COUNTRY INNS OF AMERICA

The Southwest

A GUIDE TO THE INNS OF ARIZONA, NEW MEXICO, AND TEXAS

BY ROBERTA HOMAN GARDNER
AND PETER ANDREWS

PHOTOGRAPHED BY GEORGE W. GARDNER

DESIGNED BY ROBERT REID

HOLT, RINEHART AND WINSTON, *New York*

AN OWL BOOK

Front cover: El Tovar Hotel, Grand Canyon, Arizona.
Frontispiece. An indian ceramic "Tree of Life" in the dining
   room of Lodge on the Desert.
Back cover. Indian Lodge, Fort Davis, Texas.

Map by Anthony St. Aubyn
Editing by Jim Carnes

Photographs on the following pages are used with permission
from The Knapp Press, 5900 Wilshire Blvd, LA 90036, © 1978
by Knapp Communications Corporation: 1, 26-31, 34-39, 48-
51, 60-63.

Published by Holt, Rinehart and Winston, 383 Madison
Avenue, New York, New York 10017.
Published simultaneously in Canada by Holt, Rinehart
and Winston of Canada, Limited.

Library of Congress Cataloging in Publication Data

Gardner, Roberta Homan.
   The Southwest, a guide to the inns of Arizona, New
Mexico, and Texas.
   (Country inns of America)
   (An Owl book.)
   1. Hotels, taverns, etc.—Arizona—Directories.
2. Hotels, taverns, etc.—New Mexico—Directories.
3. Hotels, taverns, etc.—Texas—Directories.
I. Andrews, Peter, 1931– . II. Gardner, George Wil-
liam, 1940– . III. Title. IV. Series.
TX907.G344   647'.947801   81-20023
ISBN 0-03-059179-1   AACR2

First Edition

10 9 8 7 6 5 4 3 2 1

A Robert Reid—Wieser & Wieser Production

Printed in the United States of America

ISBN 0-03-059179-1

THE INNS

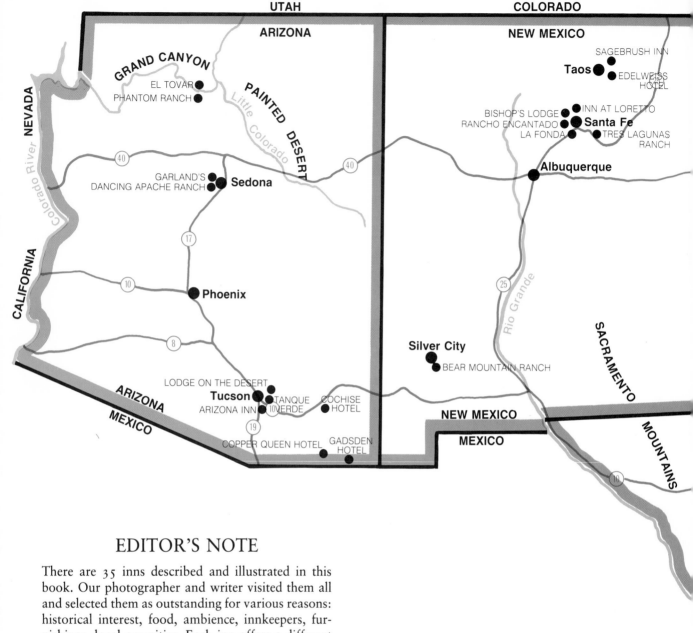

EDITOR'S NOTE

There are 35 inns described and illustrated in this book. Our photographer and writer visited them all and selected them as outstanding for various reasons: historical interest, food, ambience, innkeepers, furnishings, local amenities. Each inn offers a different mix of characteristics, so study them carefully to determine which ones you might most enjoy. All inngoers have strong personal preferences, and there are inns represented here to suit all tastes.

Visiting a country inn for the first time requires a certain spirit of adventure. Usually an inn is far nicer than we can describe it, but it is also possible for changes to occur since we were there—chefs come and go, staff changes occur—but generally these are temporary, and a visit is usually worthwhile at any time. If not, let us know. And if we have omitted some personal favorites, again let us know so that we can look at them for future editions.

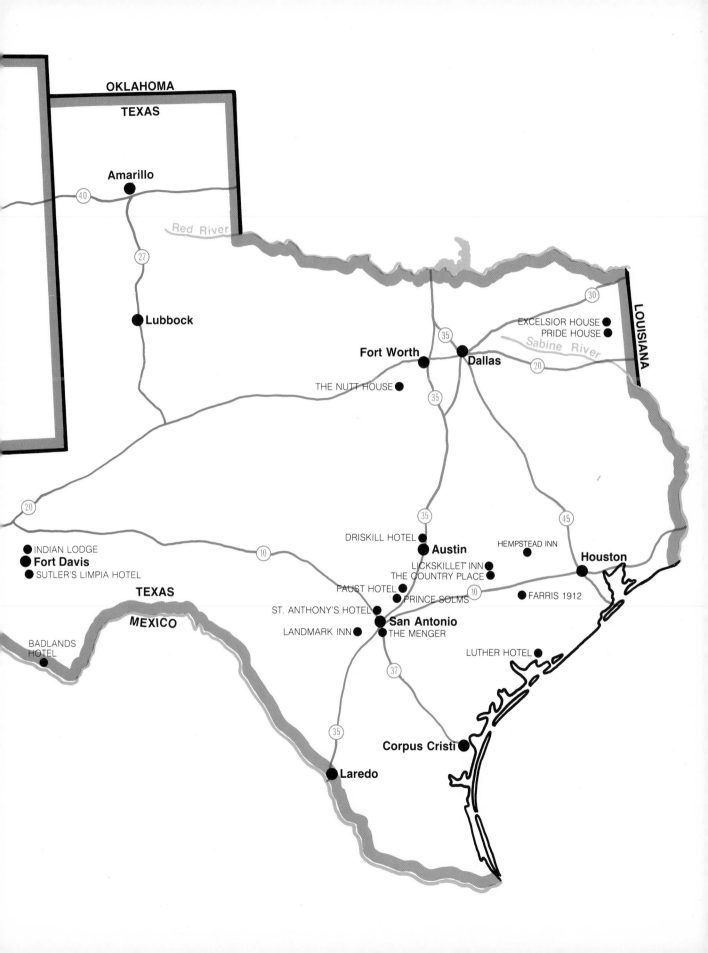

OKLAHOMA

TEXAS

Amarillo

Red River

Lubbock

Fort Worth

Dallas

LOUISIANA

EXCELSIOR HOUSE
PRIDE HOUSE

Sabine River

THE NUTT HOUSE

DRISKILL HOTEL

Austin

HEMPSTEAD INN

Houston

INDIAN LODGE
Fort Davis
SUTLER'S LIMPIA HOTEL

LICKSKILLET INN
THE COUNTRY PLACE

FAUST HOTEL
PRINCE SOLMS

FARRIS 1912

TEXAS

ST. ANTHONY'S HOTEL

San Antonio

MEXICO

LANDMARK INN

THE MENGER

BADLANDS
HOTEL

LUTHER HOTEL

Corpus Cristi

Laredo

Grand Canyon # EL TOVAR HOTEL

The Grand Canyon and civilization too

The Grand Canyon is an ancient wonder that is at once exhilarating and frightening, a natural cathedral of grand silence, filled with the sounds of the universe.

For almost a century the classic visit to this awesome spectacle has included a stay at the gracious lodge on its south rim, El Tovar. Built of massive native stone and Douglas fir imported from Oregon and styled after a Norwegian villa with touches of Swiss chalet, the inn complements the rugged and majestic terrain with astonishing ease and harmony.

Construction of the inn was initiated by Fred Harvey, the turn-of-the-century British-born hotel entrepreneur who made his reputation creating elegant Harvey Houses along the Atchison, Topeka, and Santa Fe railway line. A special attraction at the hotels were the Harvey Girls, women from "age 18 to 30, of good character, attractive, and intelligent," who were recruited from the East as lodge personnel. Though they were required to sign a contract promising to complete a one-year tour of duty, most married within six months. It is said that the Harvey Girls founded the West's first families, that approximately four thousand of the resulting male babies were named either Fred or Harvey or both, and that many prominent Westerners can trace their lineage to a Harvey Girl.

Today, though there have been such concessions to modernization as a bathroom in every room, the inn is much the same as it was when completed in 1905. The cavernous lobby is known as Rendezvous, its walls and rafters stained soft black. Trophies of native moose, elk, buffalo, peccary, deer, and antelope keep watch from the timber walls. Navajo rugs, copper hurricane lamps, a stone fireplace, and comfortable chairs invite lingering before further exploration.

A wide staircase leads to the upper lodgings. From suites, with their balcony views of the canyon, to more standard accommodations, all rooms are comfortably furnished and carpeted in warm earth colors; most beds have brass headboards; and all quarters share the luxury of a generous supply of thick, plush bath towels—a consideration much appreciated after a long day with the canyon.

The old lodge feeling is especially pervasive in the dining room; Indian murals decorate the high walls, and beautiful box lantern chandeliers cast their glow on sturdy black beams. The menu is sophisticated and thoughtful, running from eggs *cocotte* and cheese blintzes in the morning to tournedos Rossini and chicken in champagne at dinner. To dine on such fare in the middle of the desert wilderness is as delightful as it is incongruous.

But that's the charm of El Tovar. Amid one of the world's most formidable spectacles, it offers all of the comfort and luxury the austere canyon denies. And it prepares one, by so grandly lifting the spirits, for a proper descent to the depths.

EL TOVAR HOTEL, Grand Canyon National Park Lodges, Grand Canyon, Ariz. 86023; (602) 638-2631; Toby Allen, General Manager. Classic, dark-timbered western lodge of grand proportions, attentive service, and unparalleled regional flavor. Open year round. 78 guest rooms, including suites, each having private bath, tub and shower. Rates $51 to $55 per room; suites $85 to $100; children 7 and under no charge. Dining room serving three meals per day. All major credit cards accepted. No pets permitted; kennels available in park. Located in the heart of the Southwest's scenic wonders—Grand Canyon, Painted Desert, Monument Valley; Indian reservations, day and overnight hikes into canyon. Christmas at El Tovar is magical.

DIRECTIONS: Republic flies to Grand Canyon airport. From Flagstaff, take Rte. 180 north, becomes Rte. 64, which takes you directly to park. Hotel clearly marked. From Las Vegas, take I-40 east to Williams, Ariz., and I-64 interchange. Turn left onto 64 and proceed to park and hotel.

PRECEDING PAGE: El Tovar overlooking its front yard. *Left:* Rendezvous, the magnificent lobby. OVERLEAF: Each adventurer into the canyon starts off in high spirits. Right, a donkey train on the trail.

Really getting away from it all

Phantom Ranch is charged with a missionary duty: to refresh adventurers in the pursuit of wonder. A green and lush garden, it is a fitting reward for descending into the rocky depths of the Canyon.

The ranch, which has existed since 1905 when it was known as Rust Camp, is located next to the rushing waters of Bright Angel Creek in a fault that stretches across the width of the canyon. Comfortable rustic cabins, made of creekbed rock, and spotless, modern dormitories that are segregated by sex, are the available accommodations. Between cabins and dorms is a large dining hall where family style, all-you-can-eat meals are served at breakfast and dinner. Between meals the hall becomes a cafe/refreshment station. From here you can mail postcards marked "Carried by mule from Phantom Ranch."

Left: The first exciting glimpse of the bottom, and adventurers, below, enjoying the Colorado River between the rapids.

A trip into the canyon can be one of the most rewarding and uplifting experiences of a lifetime—if it is done right. Caution must be exercised; grueling is the word for the hike and rigorous for the mule ride. An overnight is necessary for all but those rare individuals who are in top physical condition. But they, too, would be wise to spend a night at the bottom, for in the evening the cottonwoods sigh in the breeze, moonflowers reveal their serene beauty, and mule deer graze unafraid. The first light of dawn illuminates blue and orange canyon walls while the emerald-hued Colorado rushes by relentlessly. It is breathtaking.

PHANTOM RANCH, Grand Canyon, Ariz. 86023; (602) 638-2401; Deborah Mahar, Manager. Rustic cabins built of boulders from the area. Open year round. 9 cabins sleeping 4 people each; 2 cabins sleeping 10 each; 4 dormitories, segregated male and female, sleeping 10 each; shared baths/shower houses. Rates $35 cabin, double occupancy; $7 for each additional; dorms $10 per bed. Restaurant serves breakfast and dinner, plus sack lunches for hikers, seven days. All major credit cards accepted. Children welcome; no pets allowed. Spectacular nature trails along Bright Angel Creek, Colorado River; fishing, with license.
DIRECTIONS: Contact Canyon park service.

Phantom Ranch amid the cottonwoods.

Sedona DANCING APACHE RANCH

ARIZONA

A home on the range in red rock country

The excitement of calf-roping on the fragrant plain; the silhouette of a lonesome cowpoke and his beloved horse against a desert sunset; the tangle of a tall tale spun beside a flickering campfire—these images stir a fascination that most of us will never outgrow. But if you believe the untamed West exists only in the movies, then mosey on down to the Dancing Apache Guest Ranch.

The ranch proper demarcates arid desert from the lush Oak Creek valley. Quarterhorses and polled Herefords graze the sprawling pastures. Two guest houses, one dating back a century and the other brand new, sit side by side in the shade of stately cottonwoods. From this vantage point, the wide-eyed greenhorn might watch Twister, and his apprentice, Bruce, breaking horses—Twister's reputation as a tamer is high and widespread, and almost daily new horses arrive for gentling by his expert hand. Or perhaps ranch manager Skeeter, his sons, and the other hands will spend the morning roping cattle in the corral. Guests are welcome to try their hand at riding and roping.

For the afternoon, a ride around the ranch with Skeeter or one of the other cowboys is popular, although a picnic by the swimming hole or angling for rainbow trout would suit a more relaxed mood.

Once acclimated to ranch life, most guests enjoy exploring neighboring Sedona or Arcosanti. Sedona offers the exquisite Tlaquepaque, a Spanish colonial village nestled under giant sycamores and filled with shops, galleries, and several fine restaurants. The red rock cliffs that surround Sedona and continue north as Oak Creek Canyon will immediately be recognized as the setting for many Western movies. Just south of Sedona is Arcosanti, architect Paoli Soleri's prototypical city which is planned for ecological responsibility and which utilizes passive solar collection for much of its energy.

Meanwhile, back at the ranch ... Patti Hughes, Skeeter's wife, has been hard at work preparing the evening's repast. An excellent cook, she nightly serves up one of her special Mexican dinners, or steaks or chicken barbecued on the grill beside the pond. Skeeter can usually be counted on for his savory

Ranch owner Jack Groves in front of a guest house.

specialties: cowboy beans—pintos that have simmered all day over the open fire—and melt-in-the-mouth skillet biscuits, which make dessert seem redundant.

As sunset fades to firelight, the memories of a day's adventures take on the glow of dreams.

DANCING APACHE GUEST RANCH, Box 2132, Sedona, Ariz. 86336; (602) 634-4524; Skeeter and Patti Hughes, Managers. A working cattle ranch offering 2 guest houses, 1 with 2 full baths and 1 with 1½ baths; each with full kitchen; up to 6 occupants per house. Rates from $200 per day, double occupancy, to $1400 per week, double; $2500 1 week, 6 occupants. Modified American plan available. Guests may bring liquor. No credit cards accepted. Children welcome; pets not encouraged, because of other animals on ranch. Famous Red Rock country; horseback riding, swimming, fishing, ranch chores; extra charge for some activities.

DIRECTIONS: From Sedona, take 89A south to Page Springs turn-off (left). Follow Page Springs Rd. approx. 2 miles, through Page Springs. Ranch is on left across Oak Creek bridge. From Phoenix, take I-17 north to Maguireville/Cornville exit. Left on Cornville Rd. approx. 10 mi. Right onto Page Springs Rd. 5 mi. to Ranch.

Left: The ranch demarcates desert from the lush Oak Creek valley. Below, lessons in roping from ranch manager Skeeter Hughes, left.

GARLAND'S LODGE

This green oasis for sophisticates is a real find

A guest at Garland's is just one of the family. This cluster of rustic, impeccably maintained cabins and central lodge nestled in the oasis of Oak Creek Valley offers a rare combination of wilderness and the familiarity of home.

High over the valley, weather-sculpted rock mountains stand watch. Two orchards surround the Lodge with some three hundred fruit trees; apples, peaches, pears, apricots, plums, and cherries are available in season. Home-grown fruits and vegetables are the hallmark of the kitchen at Garland's. "Just like Mother used to make," is its time-honored motto. For breakfast, along with the luscious fruit, guests are treated to fresh eggs from the henhouse. The home-baked bread and rolls merit superlatives with or without a topping of honey from the resident bees.

Dinner is served family style, and with the bounty of its spread, everyone is certain to excuse the occasional boardinghouse reach.

The vacationing angler will find a hearty challenge in the German Brown trout of Oak Creek. Cook your catch at sunset over an open fire.

GARLAND'S OAK CREEK LODGE, P.O. Box 152, Sedona, Ariz. 86366; (602) 282-3343; Mary and Gary Garland, Innkeepers. 11 log cabins in a lush valley, each with a porch overlooking Oak Creek. Open last weekend of March through second week of November; closed every Sunday evening. 3 small cabins with 1 double bed each; 8 large, with 2 double beds, fireplace, and sitting area. Rates $60 double in small cabin; $78 double in large; $26 each additional person in large. Rates include breakfast and dinner, served in dining room of main lodge. Visa and MasterCard credit cards accepted. Children welcome; no pets allowed. Excellent hiking and fishing in a serene mountain cul-de-sac.

DIRECTIONS: Lodge is eight miles north of Sedona on Hwy. 89A.

Loving care is lavished on grounds and guest cabins.

GADSDEN HOTEL

Shades of former glory in an Arizona cow town

From the outside it exhibits all the charm of a five-story, mint green cement block, rather unceremoniously dominating the skyline of this bicultural border town. But on entering the Gadsden prepare to be astonished. The main staircase, in solid white Italian marble, sweeps to the second floor balcony. Grand pillars of pink marble, each topped with a gilt pediment, support a ceiling bejeweled with two signed Tiffany skylights. A stained glass mural depicting the Western landscape sweeps the length of one wall.

Though the food is commonplace and accommodations edge toward seediness, the hotel lobby is a great place for people-watching. All types are drawn to the Gadsden, from a grab bag of permanent residents, to writers, cattle barons, cowboys, and actors on location. The hotel watering hole, just outside the lobby limelight, is the Saddle and Spur saloon; its walls are decorated with over two hundred registered cattle brands, and its clientele wore cowboy hats long before "country" was chic.

Constructed of wood in 1907, the original hotel was destroyed by fire in 1928. Rebuilt one year later in concrete and steel, the Gadsden is on the National Register of Historic Buildings and stands alone, in this wide open cow town, in serendipitous glory.

THE GADSDEN HOTEL, 1046 G Ave., Douglas, Ariz. 85607; (602) 364-2411; C. James Nolan, Innkeeper. The contrast between this building's green cement exterior and its jewel-like grand lobby is startling; a focal point of regional activity. Open year round. 160 guest rooms, including suites and apartments, all with private baths, tub/shower. Rates range from around $20 single to $65 for Governor's Suite; $4 roll-away charge. Restaurant serves three meals, seven days. All major credit cards accepted, including foreign. Children and pets welcome. Two dances a week—live western swing music; border crossing to Agua Prieta, Mex.

DIRECTIONS: From El Paso, take 80 west to Douglas; Hotel is on 80 (which becomes G St. in town). From Tucson, I-10 east to Rte. 80, into Douglas.

The Tiffany ceiling, supported by carved marble columns.

COPPER QUEEN HOTEL

Accommodations come in all shapes and sizes

The yawning, thousand-foot-deep Lavender Pit welcomes your arrival. A silent relic of past prosperity, it sprawls in rich sunset hues and sculpted dimensions at once startlingly beautiful and terrible.

After mining all but ceased here in the 1970s, Bisbee came within a hair's breadth of becoming a ghost town. This was one of the greatest copper camps in the world, beginning in 1880 with the Glory Hole, and moving on to the fabulously rich Copper Queen and the Lavender open-pit mine. Bisbee become a fortune hunter's dream and contracted all the symptoms of prosperity. The local brewery slaked a boundless thirst and Brewery Gulch was chock-a-block with sixty-eight saloons and sixty-seven brothels. But wealth brought taste and culture as well, most notably in the form of an opera house and the Copper Queen Hotel. The most prominent building in town—cream stucco with red brick trim, a pillared, moss green balcony porch, and red tile roof—the Copper Queen exudes the charm of a classic Northern Italian resort hotel.

Inside, the lobby epitomizes Western elegance; its atmosphere, enveloped in dark and lustrous woodwork, is decidedly masculine. Cranberry glass lamps, their prisms casting splashes of color, brighten the darkness of the brown upholstered easy chairs, the original check-in desk, and a broad central staircase. To the left and through double screen doors, the dining room, also of dark wood but enlivened with blue-and-white checkered tablecloths and a stained glass screen, offers three generous and delicious meals a day. At dinner, after a starter of cheese and relishes, you might enjoy a fine rendition of roast duck *à*

l'orange, skillet chicken, or German-style potato pancakes served with a thick and succulent ham steak. For those who have saved room, a slice of fresh-baked apple pie *à la mode* or French cheesecake is the perfect finale.

Accommodations come in all shapes and sizes, from cozy cubbyholes to a suite spacious enough to satisfy John Wayne when he was a guest. The rooms, in their simplicity and cleanliness, are reassuring remembrances of a less sophisticated time.

Artists and craftspeople are increasingly attracted to Bisbee and its unique "faded glory" character. With this influx of creative people have come many shops and galleries and a fine selection of used book stores. Mine tours, guided by old-time miners who explain in detail "the way it was," are fascinating. To all this add a splendid mountain climate, just north of the Mexican border, and you have got one of the best vacation spots the Southwest has to offer.

COPPER QUEEN HOTEL, P.O. Drawer CQ, 11 Howell St., Bisbee, Ariz. 85603; (602) 432-2216; Virginia and Richard Hort, Innkeepers. Handsome red brick Italianate structure with broad porches, sheet copper detailing. Open year round. Forty-five guest rooms (by 1982), each with private bath, tub or shower. Rates from $22 to $37 double, varying with size and view. Saloon and restaurant with patio serving three meals per day, open to public and guests. Children welcome; pets not allowed. Visa and MasterCard credit cards accepted. Swimming pool on premises; tennis courts nearby. Old copper boom town rich in Wild West history; mine tours, museums, numerous bookstores and arts & crafts galleries.

DIRECTIONS: From Tucson, take I-10 east to Benson. Exit right and take 80 to Bisbee. Exit right into Bisbee business district. Hotel is visible from highway. From El Paso (4½ hours), take I-10 west to Wilcox exit. Take Rte. 666 south to Rte. 80, and 80 into Bisbee.

Left: The Copper Queen lobby is "elegance, western style."

A mirage that turns out to be real

"Never judge a book by its cover." The old adage could well serve as the motto of the Cochise Hotel. The dry wind whistles through the streets of the town as if in a classic Western. The imaginative traveler keeps a sharp eye peeled for a six-shooter or a lonesome tumbleweed. The dusty hotel appears deserted, as befits the scene. But a second glance reveals a white picket fence at the rear, and a walkway marked with a neat currant hedge. Innkeeper Lillie Harrington likes to keep an eye on the comings and goings of her guests, so the front door is kept locked; traffic moves through the kitchen.

First-timers at the Cochise would swear they had walked into a mirage. The assortment of antiques housed in this plain building is breathtaking. Two ten-foot-long solid oak and mahogany veneer tables command the dining room. Three mirrored sideboards, an etched-glass chandelier, a wall cabinet brimming with china treasures, and sepia photographs of local homesteaders complete the tableau. Just beyond, spears of hollyhock rustle the screens of the enclosed porch. In the formal living room oil portraits preside over an upright piano and a gold velvet settee, and assorted armchairs surround an Oriental rug mellowed by time and Tiffany lamplight.

The entire collection of furnishings, including the period pieces that stock the bedrooms, was shipped west from Waterbury, Connecticut, by the present owner of the Cochise, Mrs. Thomas B. Husband. Originally from Waterbury but raised in the West, she heard that the hotel, whose business had been languishing for some time, was to be converted into a produce warehouse. An abiding concern for the preservation of Western landmarks spurred her purchase. She opened a gift shop behind the hotel and asked Lillie to manage the establishment for her.

The parlor wardrobe.

The traveler should be wise, however, to a word of warning. Lillie can be a bit cantankerous—after all, she's one of the ladies who helped tame this wild land. Guests can count on delicious homemade breakfast and dinner, but they'll be served on Lillie's terms. Dinner entrées include a choice of chicken or steak, and whoever orders first orders for everyone because she won't do both on the same night. By the way, when Lillie says, "Dinner's at seven, and the same goes for breakfast," she means it. Latecomers should expect a cold meal.

That's all, podners.

Left: above, the front porch faces train tracks on the desert plain. Below, a view from the dining room of the parlor settee, reputed to have belonged to Jenny Lind. OVERLEAF: The barren exterior of this former Wells Fargo office belies the inn's interior charms.

COCHISE HOTEL, Cochise, Ariz. 85606; (602) 384-3156; Elizabeth Husband, Innkeeper. A 1-story white adobe inn in a tiny town. Open year round. 3 double rooms and 2 suites, sleeping a total of 12. Rates $12 single; $15 double; suites $20. Two meals served daily in the dining room. Children not encouraged; no pets allowed. Liquor not served but permitted. No credit cards accepted.

DIRECTIONS: From Tucson, take I-10 east, right onto 666, 5½ miles to sign for Cochise, turn right to hotel.

TANQUE VERDE RANCH

Tucson   ARIZONA

The emphasis is on riding and luxury

The dude ranch is an extraordinary phenomenon that could only have developed in America. Nobody is exactly sure who was responsible for the idea, but most credit usually goes to author Owen Wister. Harvard educated, Wister spent several summers in Wyoming for his health and fell in love with the western frontier. His stories and books, particularly his most famous novel, *The Virginian,* published in 1903, fascinated armchair travelers in the East. Before long, tenderfoots were flocking to ranches in the West and were actually paying money to work as cowboys so they could experience firsthand the kind of life that Wister had so effectively described.

Tanque Verde, founded by Rafael Carillo on a Spanish land grant in 1862, is one of the oldest ranches in America now being used as a guest facility.

The ranch is one of the most luxurious of country inns, featuring indoor and outdoor swimming pools, whirlpool baths, air-conditioned rooms, and a dining room whose chef likes to whip up such desserts as mocha marzipan torte.

The emphasis is on riding, so much so that unlimited horseback riding is included in the room rate. The ranch has more than eighty horses and three full-time wranglers. Most of the social program of the ranch revolves around trail riding. In the morning, for example, guests may ride to breakfast at the old abandoned hut up the road and afterwards take to the trails for the second ride of the day.

The few who don't want to ride that day can spend their time rallying on the ranch's private tennis courts, playing golf at one of the six championship courses nearby, or just snoozing in a hammock, waiting for the next barbecue.

The guest rooms and suites are all ranch-style, with low beamed ceilings and brick walls. Most of the rooms have their own adobe fireplaces and all lead out onto their own private lounging area. The main building, which was built in the early 1870s, is a

Western ease and comfort characterize accommodations.

solid, L-shaped ranch house with walls almost two feet thick. One of the most popular spots is the Dog House Bar, where guests can bring their own liquor and are given a small locker in which to keep it.

In the evening the sound of the birds and the voices of the wind in the leaves of the quaking aspens give way to the awesome silence of Grand View, with mountain peaks stretching out for miles above the hushed valley below. Each guest room then looks out on another world—the magnificent Old West.

Left: The stonework around the pool adds drama to an already spectacular landscape of 1,500,000 acres of untarnished wilderness. OVERLEAF: Typical Spanish ranch architecture. *Following pages:* A few of the inn's 85 horses, used for riding among the saguaro cactus on the breathtaking desert trails.

TANQUE VERDE RANCH, Rte. 8, Box 66, Tucson, Ariz. 85710; (602) 296-6275; Bob Cote, Innkeeper. Sixty secluded cottages in the foothills of the Rincon Mountains. Open year round. Room rates vary with the season and the accommodation, and all include meals and horseback riding privileges. Through Dec. 15, 1981 $70 to $100 single; $99 to $135 double. Restaurant serves meals to guests only. No credit cards accepted. Indoor and outdoor pools, tennis, sauna.

DIRECTIONS: Take the Speedway all the way to the end. Inn is on the left.

LODGE ON THE DESERT

Tucson   **ARIZONA**

A lush, quiet corner of Shangri-la.

Words waft from a neighboring table, "This is my favorite place ... it's my hideaway." Unsolicited testimonials from longtime guests are commonplace at The Lodge on the Desert. The Lodge is within the city limits of Tucson, but its quiet, secluded grounds might as easily be a corner of Shangri-la.

An adobe wall surrounds lush acreage that feels, for all the world, like a botanical garden. Walkways wind through the shade and aroma of sweet oleander, mock orange, date palms, barrel cactus, mesquite, and agave, to name but a few of the species nurtured by a full-time gardener. Within the garden maze are scattered eleven adobe-style casas; on the face of each cottage, the patterned shadows of ocotillo awnings mark the slow passage of the sun. The center of the garden is a luxuriant lawn that sweeps grandly up to the main lodge. A shuffleboard court, ping-pong tables, and a heated swimming pool framed by graceful palms offer diversion along this promenade.

Rooms range from "standard," meaning clean, comfortable, and cozy, to "elegant," meaning exactly that. The latter accommodations include either their own private sun deck or a swimming pool, a living room decorated in warm tones of peach and cream, a walk-in closet, and a bathroom fit for visiting royalty.

Floor-to-ceiling windows in the Lodge's dining room and bar open onto a picturesque patio, where a fountain and lily pond set the peaceful tone. Choose a table to suit your mood, in front of a fireplace, in a dark and private corner, or under an umbrella in the vivid garden. After lunch you might want to take your coffee into the lounge, where game tables, a well-stocked library of books and magazines, and a herd of perfectly overstuffed chairs comprise a haven for those idle hours.

An outing in Tucson is a must during a stay at the Lodge. San Xavier Mission, Kitt Peak Observatory, and the Sonoran Desert Museum are three favorite sights. Tennis, swimming, golf, or horseback riding on desert trails fill out an invigorating schedule.

The Lodge on the Desert is a harmony of details, and one small example is a special favorite: leave an order outside your door before retiring, and next morning a breakfast tray will be served with a smile.

Left: The grounds are set up for outdoor relaxation.

The main lodge is luxury Spanish Western.

How better to ensure the start of another fine day in the old pueblo, Tucson.

THE LODGE ON THE DESERT, P.O. Box 42500, 306 N. Alvernon Way, Tucson, Ariz. 85733; (602) 325-3366; Schuyler W. Lininger, patron grande. Individual pueblo-style casas situated in enclosed garden grounds. Open year round. Eleven groupings of casas with two or more rooms each, thirty-eight guest rooms in all; private baths throughout, tub or shower. Rates, including continental breakfast, $60 to $142 double, Nov. 1 to May 1; $40 to $91 double, May 1 to Nov. 1. Dining room serves breakfast, lunch, and dinner, seven days. Children welcome; pets on leash permitted. Visa and MasterCard credit cards accepted. Ample recreation on grounds or nearby—swimming, golf, tennis, racquetball, shuffleboard. Surrounded by 4 mountain ranges.

DIRECTIONS: From Tucson Intl. Airport, drive east on Valencia, turn left onto Palo Verde, which becomes Alvernon. Approx. 3 miles from Valencia St. to Lodge. From southern California, take I-10 east to Speedway exit. Go east on Speedway approx. 4.5 miles to Alvernon. Turn right, going south, 3 blocks to inn. From southern Texas, take I-10 west to Palo Verde exit. Stay right on Palo Verde, which becomes Alvernon, to Lodge.

ARIZONA INN

Tucson

Simplicity and grandeur over 14 lush acres

A sumptuous corner of the main lounge.

It is appropriate that a place as gracious as the Arizona Inn should have come about as the result of an act of compassion by a kind lady. Isabella Greenway came from a family prominent in Eastern society and was a bridesmaid at the wedding of Franklin and Eleanor Roosevelt. Later moving to Arizona, she became a noted rancher, artist, and the only congresswoman in the history of the state. In 1927 she founded a handicraft shop to create jobs for unemployed World War I veterans, who were put to work making western-style furniture. Unfortunately the Great Depression of 1929 knocked the bottom out of the business. Mrs. Greenway, not having the heart to tell her ex-soldiers to stop, created this spacious country resort to have a place for the furniture they were making.

Adding a mixture of her own family heirlooms and antiques along with some fine examples of contemporary Mexican-American crafts, Mrs. Greenway opened the inn in 1930 as a hideaway for her wealthy friends. For many years the John D. Rockefeller family wintered here, and the inn's swimming pool was largely added so that young Nelson and David would have a place to splash about in. Winston Churchill, Salvador Dali, Cary Grant, and the Duke and Duchess of Windsor were all once guests at the inn.

Although the resort is considerably more relaxed under the present ownership of Mrs. Greenway's son John, there is still an air of Old World gentility about the inn. General manager Robert Minerich supervises an unusually large staff—including twenty gardeners—who take care of the eighty-six pleasant cottage rooms.

The inn itself is made of a soft coral adobe highlighted by shutters and trim of a brisk Williamsburg blue. The public rooms are baronial, made charmingly intimate by light western touches. The library is big, comfortable, and high-ceilinged, and the bar is a visual delight. Open and sunny, it is a study in soft beige and gray, accented by a huge central skylight.

Bud Judd is the remarkable new chef in charge of the spacious dining room, which has acquired such a high reputation that many people make the two-hour drive from Phoenix just to come to dinner. The menu is continental, with a few individual flourishes such as the Arizona Inn Special: eggplant sauteed with medallions of tenderloin and artichoke hearts. When more and more restaurants are relying on precooked, preprocessed, and frozen foods, the kitchen at the inn still prepares everything from scratch.

"The giants of the industry say that a place like this can't exist," says Robert Minerich. "Well, we're out to prove them wrong."

Left: The library is carpeted with soft, lush Moroccan rugs. OVERLEAF: a rear view of the low-lying inn. *Following pages:* the pleasant dining room and the skylighted bar.

ARIZONA INN, 2200 East Elm St., Tucson, Ariz. 85719; (602) 325-1541; Robert Minerich, Innkeeper. An 86-room inn, located on 14 acres near the University of Arizona campus in suburban Tucson. Open year round. Rates Jan. through April $64 to $90 single, $74 to $100 double; May through Aug. $41 to $58 single, $51 to $66 double; Sept. through Dec. $50 to $64 single, $65 to $79 double. Private and shared baths. Restaurant serves breakfast, lunch, and dinner. American Express, MasterCard, Visa and Carte Blanche credit cards accepted. Heated swimming pool, tennis courts, putting green and badminton.

DIRECTIONS: From I-10, take Speedway Blvd. east to the University of Arizona. Turn left on Campbell; five blocks down, turn right onto East Elm.

SAGEBRUSH INN

Taos   NEW MEXICO

Introducing . . . Ken and Louise Blair

"There's a saying in Taos that if the mountain doesn't like you, you won't stay long," says Ken Blair, owner of the Sagebrush Inn. "If you come here to change Taos, you won't make it. You must accept the place as it is, and you must be for it."

The population mix in Taos is ninety percent Spanish and Indian and ten percent Anglo (meaning whites, blacks, and Orientals). It's a rare Anglo establishment that draws support from the locals, but Ken is for Taos, and in turn Taos is for the Sagebrush.

The inn dates back to 1929, when the carriage trade between New York and Arizona was flourishing. Local workmen hauled the huge kiva beams from the surrounding Sangre de Cristo Mountains, and women laid the handmade adobe bricks to a thickness of twenty-four inches. During World War II the inn was leased to a boys' school, and from that time the building began a slow decline that ended in 1974, when Ken bought it for restoration.

"The place was literally falling apart. Plaster was coming off the walls, and there were terrible leaks. At first I felt the place had gone too far, that there was no way to restore it. But as things worked out, I bought it anyway." A native of Massachusetts, Ken moved to Taos in 1973, leaving behind a successful, conventional career. "My friends back home can't understand how I could give up all I had there to live in a desert. Easterners think that's all New Mexico is," he chuckles.

A Sagebrush visitor entering the inn for the first time might think he had entered the parlor of a reclusive art patron. Reclusive Ken is not, but much of the inn's vast collection of Southwestern art he did obtain in return for aid to local artists during cash-flow dry spells. The evidence of his generosity-cum-foresight gives the Sagebrush a unique sophistication and vitality.

In their dimensions and decor, the lodgings reflect the inn's meandering history. From the original, tiny rooms to brand new, spacious suites, each has a cozy beehive fireplace, which is laid with piñon pine each morning. The colors throughout are quietly evocative: soft tans, browns, and lava black. You might ask for the room Georgia O'Keefe painted in during a lengthy stay at the inn.

Left: Innkeepers Louise and Ken Blair and friend in their adobe hacienda.

The Blairs' art collection includes several exquisite Navajo rugs.

Ken and his vivacious wife, Louise, set the tone at the Sagebrush. They are generous, they enjoy themselves, and the spirit is infectious. The Sagebrush is like Taos itself: the first glance reveals a disheveled charm. A longer look reveals layers of inner beauty.

SAGEBRUSH INN, P.O. Box 1566, S. Santa Fe Rd., Taos, N. Mex. 87571; (505) 758-2254; Ken and Louise Blair, Innkeepers. Rambling, pueblo-style inn that doubles as a gallery for the Blair's extensive collection of Southwestern art. Open year round. Sixty-three guest rooms, each with private bath. Rates from $35 single and $40 double to $55 for suites. Dining room and separate dinner theater serving two meals per day, Sept. through May; lunch also, June—Aug. All major credit cards accepted. Children and pets welcome. Jacuzzi, swimming pool, and tennis courts on premises. Taos/Santa Fe area offers spectacular scenery, myriad art galleries, historic sites, and outdoor activities, all with a rich regional flavor.

DIRECTIONS: From Santa Fe, 68 north to Taos. Inn is on left of 68 approaching Taos. From Denver, take I-25 south to Raton. Just past Raton, exit onto Rt. 64 and drive west to Taos. 64 turns left at first stoplight. Turn and follow 64 south to Sagebrush.

Taos # HOTEL EDELWEISS

Alpine hospitality in Taos, New Mexico

Its name conveys the essence of the Hotel Edelweiss—European hospitality in an alpine setting of snowy peaks, crystalline air, and shimmering mountain flowers. According to many international sportsmen, the Taos Ski Valley of the Sangre de Cristo Mountains affords the closest thing to true alpine skiing in the United States. Innkeepers Dadou and Ilse Mayer have made certain that their hostelry lives up to the region's lofty claim.

The shingle-roofed stucco and timber structure comprises sixteen immaculate and cozy guest rooms, and a detached cabin offers four more. In the communal den, a crackling fire dispels the chill of the slopes and casts a warm glow on memories of spills and triumphs.

The Mayer family is dedicated to European excellence. Guest rates include three meals per day—breakfast, cooked by Dadou himself, at the Edelweiss dining room, with lunch and dinner at the Hotel St. Bernard next door. Managed by Dadou's brother Jean, the St. Bernard maintains a world class reputation for its French gourmet cuisine. The menu changes daily, with specialties ranging from lobster Newburg to duck *à l'orange*.

In its perfect semblance of a quaint alpine inn, the Edelweiss also offers the more contemporary luxuries of jacuzzi, sauna, and tennis courts on the grounds. Secluded in the mountains just nineteen miles north of Taos, the Edelweiss is as rare and cheering as its namesake.

HOTEL EDELWEISS, Taos Ski Valley, N. Mex. 87571; (505) 776-2301; Dadou and Ilse Mayer, Innkeepers. Stucco and timber European style chalet. Open two seasons—Thanksgiving to Easter, and June 15 to August 31. Sixteen guest rooms and one 4-bedroom cabin. Rates, including 3 meals per day, $90 single in winter, $55 summer; $75 per person double in winter, $85 for 2, summer; special children's rate. Hotel dining room, with some meals served at Hotel St. Bernard next door. No credit cards, but personal checks accepted. No pets allowed. Tennis court, jacuzzi, and sauna on premises; alpine skiing, hiking trails; fishing.
DIRECTIONS: 130 miles north of Albuquerque, 19 miles north of Taos, in Taos Ski Valley.

The inn, and its mountain setting.

Unfailingly consistent cheer and efficiency

The Inn at Loretto is noteworthy for two reasons: first, it is one of the loveliest mission-style buildings in all of Santa Fe, and second, from desk clerks to chambermaids, it operates with unfailingly consistent cheer and efficiency. And if it is more impersonal than most inns, it is also more diverse. Rather like a little-big hotel, the lobby shelters a variety of sophisticated shops—from wine, cheese, and gourmet foods, to fine jewelry and Southwest Indian art. Another plus is location. Situated next to the Loretto Chapel, famed for its lovely and mysterious staircase, and between the historic plaza and Canyon Drive, which is a shopper's mecca, the hotel is superbly placed for exploring the many delights of this "City Different," as the natives call Santa Fe.

The interior atmosphere is cool and relaxing; care was taken to decorate in the southwest style, but with inventiveness. Thus, the inn commissioned a potter to create simple thrown cylinders of unglazed clay to serve as the common lighting fixtures and in the dining room the regulation tin lamp has become a chandelier with slender tin feathers hanging in graceful profusion. Authentic Indian symbols, painted in bold medallions, decorate the walls throughout.

INN AT LORETTO, 211 Old Santa Fe Trail, Santa Fe, N. Mex. 87501; (505) 988-5531; John F. Sexton, General Manager; James Bagby, Executive Assistant Manager. Pueblo style inn of recent vintage. Open year round. One hundred and thirty-nine guest rooms, each with private bath. Rates available on request. Children under twelve no charge. Coffee shop serves three meals per day; formal dining room dinner only. Children welcome; pets discouraged. All major credit cards accepted. Children's playground and outdoor heated pool on premises. Conveniently located in the heart of picturesque Santa Fe. Free pick-up at Santa Fe airport; two days' notice appreciated.

DIRECTIONS: From Albuquerque, take I-25 north to State Rte. 285 (exit #284). Turn left onto Old Pecos Trail. Follow road approximately 3½ miles to Inn. From Denver, take I-25 south to State Rte. 285 (exit #284). See directions above.

The entrance to the inn is boldly beautiful.

THE BISHOP'S LODGE

Santa Fe   **NEW MEXICO**

An atmosphere of casual charm and total relaxation

The main lodge.

Complexity masked as carefree simplicity, The Bishop's Lodge makes all seem easy. From an intricate recipe of activities and services, classic accommodations, first-rate kitchen, rich history, and a dash of secret mountain essence, here is brewed an atmosphere of casual charm and total relaxation.

In the early seventeenth century a group of Franciscan friars discovered the site and found its temperate climate ideal for fruit growing. In the mid-1800s Archbishop John Lamy, who was the inspiration for Willa Cather's novel *Death Comes to the Archbishop,* was sent to Santa Fe and became enchanted with the old orchard's setting. He purchased the property, converted an existing ranch house into his personal retreat, added a chapel, and planted the winding gardens still tended today.

After Lamy's death the Sisters of Loretto sold the retreat to Joseph Pulitzer, who proceeded to construct two spacious adobe homes for his daughters. In 1918 James R. Thorpe, a Denver mining man, bought the compound and started a guest ranch, opening the Pulitzer homes and the Archbishop's charming chapel and gardens to the public.

Today James Jr. operates The Bishop's Lodge with finesse. Each impeccably clean guest room entices with the fresh aroma of citrus zest, and each is decorated in soft earth shades that mimic the mountains and valleys surrounding the lodge. While some quarters are reminiscent of a cozy country house, others reflect their southwestern heritage in beehive fireplaces and rugged kiva beams.

In his search for a fine chef, Thorpe found a Swiss jewel. Every day of the week masterful renditions of continental and New Mexican specialties are served up. The Sunday brunch, which includes pâtés, fresh crab and salmon, an extravagant selection of salads, fresh fruits, hot meats and vegetables, and a table laden with rich desserts concocted by the inspired pastry chef, is a feast that earns raves and a loyal following.

The lodge thoughtfully provides a range of activities to help utilize those mega-calories. You may feel drawn to the Olympic-size pool, or to horseback riding on the thousand-acre private grounds. Hiking and running trails crisscross the rolling mountainside. Trap and skeet shooting, a game of tennis or instructions from the full-time pro, fishing in the stocked pond or in the clear mountains streams nearby, or a relaxing game of shuffleboard fill out the agenda. A day or two in Santa Fe, browsing through galleries, shops, and museums, is a must. All of this can be topped off with a luxurious escape to the jacuzzi or sauna to smooth out muscles and to prepare for the upcoming day.

Each season at The Bishop's Lodge brings its own beauty: summer is the peak season with all activities in full swing and a battalion of trained counselors to care for kids from dawn to dusk; spring and autumn offer a more contemplative beauty, a prime bonus being that both lodge and town are free from the bustle of the summer throng.

Left: The fabulous grounds contain a profusion of Santa Fe's celebrated spring lilacs.

THE BISHOP'S LODGE, P.O. Box 2367, Sante Fe, N. Mex. 87501; (505) 983-6377; James R. Thorpe, Jr., Innkeeper. Five pueblo buildings comprising sixty units from conventional hotel doubles to deluxe suites. Open roughly March to November; may vary according to occupancy. Rates from $64 standard double to $125 deluxe suite in spring and fall; summer American plan June 1 through Labor Day $132 double to $185 deluxe suite. Restaurant serves breakfast and lunch buffet, dinner from menu. No credit cards, but personal checks accepted. No pets allowed. Children welcome—complete activities and meals program for children and for teenagers. Beautiful mountain garden setting; excellent hiking, sightseeing in the heart of Old New Mexico.

DIRECTIONS: From the north via U.S. 285, turn onto Old Taos Hwy, left at Paseo de Peralta, then left onto Bishop's Lodge Rd. From south, take 85 north to St. Francis Dr., right to Paseo de Peralta, then Bishop's Lodge Rd.

A magnetic attraction for the entire city

A pair of the many unique bedsteads.

"The inn at the end of the Santa Fe Trail." The words conjure up visions of mystery and romance, shadows by firelight, the soft strains of a Spanish guitar. Yet two centuries before that trail was even blazed there was a *fonda,* the Spanish word for inn, mentioned in a document of 1610 describing the new Royal City of Santa Fe.

Through the years the inn has played host to a cavalcade of fascinating characters, who left a colorful history in their wake. Visitors passing through its carved wooden doors have included President Rutherford B. Hayes, General Ulysses S. Grant, Kit Carson, Billy the Kid, (who, as the story goes, washed dishes in the kitchen), and a stream of pioneers, traders, merchants, trappers, politicians, gamblers, and soldiers.

The structure is a rambling Spanish-style adobe that dominates a city block. Like many big-city hotels, it houses on the first floor a *galleria* of specialty shops, offering a variety of goods from flowers, imported toiletries, and candy to exotic rugs. Central to the lobby is La Plazuela, the main restaurant, serving regional and continental fare amid a profusion of plants and flowers. The floor is paved in irregular stone slabs, the ceiling is skylighted, and traditional carving and rough-hewn beams add a rustic warmth and charm. The walls of the restaurant are actually windowed doors, each pane of which is handpainted in the southwestern version of stained glass.

Guest rooms are vibrant with handpainted furnishings, Mexican tin lamps, colorfully tiled bathrooms, and Indian graphics. To make matters perfect, the mattresses are heavenly comfortable.

One-half block from the historic town plaza, the inn's location is ideal for exploring Santa Fe. The plaza is designated a National Historic Landmark—from 1822 to 1879 it marked the end of the Santa Fe Trail. Today it is the site of the popular Indian market held every August, and the Arts and Crafts Fair in September. Across from the plaza is the Palace of Governors, which was built between 1610 and 1612 and is the oldest government building in the United States. From the palace you will be drawn into the art district for which the city is famous. Nearly a hundred galleries exhibit painting, sculpture, and prints, as well as antique and contemporary crafts. The Santa Fe Opera, several fine museums, and an active theater make Santa Fe the Southwest's cultural mecca.

Santa Fe attracts interesting people from all walks of life, and the lobby of La Fonda provides a ringside seat from which to observe this ebb and flow—somehow this inn's magnetic attraction draws the entire city to it.

LA FONDA, 100 E. San Francisco St., Santa Fe, N. Mex. 87501; (505) 982-5511; Gordon Barto, Innkeeper. Historic landmark building in pueblo adobe style; colorful regional decor throughout. Open year round. One hundred seventy rooms ranging from singles to two-bedroom suites, all with private bath. Rates $64 to $70 single; $74 to $80 double; suites $125 to $225; $10 per extra occupant; special off-season (Oct.—Apr.) ski packages available. Children under 12 free. La Plazuela, enclosed courtyard restaurant, serves three meals per day. All major credit cards accepted. Pets not encouraged. Wide range of recreational facilities available on premises or nearby. Ideally located in the heart of Old Santa Fe.

DIRECTIONS: From Albuquerque, take I-25 north to Cerillos Rd. exit to Santa Fe. Stay on Cerillos to Galesteo St. at the Capitol bldg. Stay on Galesteo to San Francisco, turn right—2 blocks to hotel. From Denver: Take I-25 south to Paseo de Peralta Dr. exit. Turn left and stay on Paseo de Peralta to Washington, then Washington to plaza. Circle right to San Francisco, turn left—1 block to La Fonda.

Left: The lobby is a traditional Santa Fe meeting spot. The guest rooms are all colorfully and exquisitely decorated.

RANCHO ENCANTADO

Tesuque　　　　　　　　　　　　　　　　　　　　NEW MEXICO

Adobe luxury in Chaparral country

Only eight miles from Santa Fe, Rancho Encantado is a secluded complex in the chaparral country of New Mexico. Its heavily beamed roofs and adobe walls would have been the pride of any sixteenth-century conquistador. Actually, Rancho Encantado is a modern, highly sophisticated hotel operation that in just twelve years has become one of the premier resort facilities in America while still retaining the atmosphere and amenities of an old southwestern ranch.

The original structure was built around 1929, and until 1967 the ranch was a small country hotel with twelve rooms and two cottages. It was then that the energetic Betty Egan bought the place and set about transforming it. She expanded the main building and added more cottages. Each accommodation at Rancho Encantado is scrupulously faithful to the traditional adobe ranch style. Made of adobe, brick, and hand-painted tile, the rooms are decorated with authentic Indian rugs, wall hangings, and art objects from the area. Most of the rooms have their own patios, affording a magnificent vista of the Sangre de Cristo and Jemez mountains. Mrs. Egan has added tennis courts, a swimming pool, and a stable and corral for the rancho's own herd of riding horses.

The decor of the charming, multilevel adobe restaurant matches the choice of traditional southwestern dishes such as *huevos rancheros* and *chiles rel-*

Magnificent artifacts of the Spanish Colonial period are displayed throughout the inn.

lenos, but guests also have a choice of international cuisine.

"We call ourselves a guest ranch rather than a dude ranch," Mrs. Egan explains. By whatever label, Rancho Encantado, with its comfortable elegance and conscientious service, has developed a loyal clientele who usually have to make reservations far in advance for its sixty accommodations. Some come for the riding and the summer sports. Some prefer to go sightseeing along the same trails first made by men who came here more than four hundred years ago searching for "gold, glory, and God." Others just enjoy the food and relax in the warm New Mexico sunshine.

Like all personally run operations, Rancho Encantado is an extension of its innkeeper. As Betty Egan says: "We are not a hotel in the usual sense; each room is furnished differently. We keep everything on a personal level. I get to know each of our guests— and our guests all get to know each other. There is a spirit of hospitality in the Southwest that's summed up in the expression, *'Mi casa, su casa,'* which means, 'My house is your house.' That's the way we feel here."

One of the guest rooms, with its fireplace and beamed ceiling.

Left: Typical of the Southwest are chilies drying in the sun. The gateway illustrates the adobe construction of the inn, shown OVERLEAF in its setting, the ruggedly beautiful New Mexico countryside.

RANCHO ENCANTADO, P.O. Box, 570, Santa Fe, N. Mex. 87501; (505) 982-3537; Betty Egan, Innkeeper. A 28-room ranch resort in the New Mexico Chaparral country. Open from shortly after Easter to early January, depending on the weather. Room rates average $85 double occupancy; cottages and suites available. Restaurant serves breakfast, lunch, and dinner. All major credit cards accepted. Tennis courts, swimming pool, shooting range, horseback riding.

DIRECTIONS: Take I-84 north from Santa Fe to the Tesuque exit. Take N.M. 22 past Tesuque about 2 miles to inn sign on right. The inn is a mile down the road.

PHOTOGRAPHED BY STEVE NORTHUP

TRES LAGUNAS RANCH
Pecos   **NEW MEXICO**

Home to travelers in the Pecos wilderness

Tucked snugly in the canyons of the Sangre de Cristo Mountains and bordered by the rushing Pecos River, Tres Lagunas Guest Ranch calls the wilderness its home. But the comforts of this cul-de-sac would tempt even Pecos Bill himself to swear off roughing it.

The front porch of the main lodge, complete with porch swing, is shaded by looming Ponderosa pines. Enter through the massive front doorway into the living room, where matching floor-to-ceiling stone fireplaces, television, bar, and a small library of Westerns and nature guidebooks invite relaxation, both solitary and social; the dining room just beyond offers a picture-window panorama of the legendary Pecos River.

Each of the out-cabins has its own sitting porch, where mountain fragrances and cushioned chairs make the rat race impossible to remember or imagine. Inside, rustic timber-and-mortar walls and beamed ceilings capture the flavor of the region. A fireplace in each cabin is laid every morning, since the mountain altitude makes for crisp evenings even in summer. Wall-to-wall carpeting and clawfoot bathtubs complete the cozy scene.

Meals, which are included in the price of a stay, are heralded by a dinner bell that sounds across this canyon meadow. Each day brings a special dinner—one entree for all—which might include barbecued steak, a Mexican or Italian spread, trout, or roast beef. Salad lovers are delighted to find an all-you-

The guest cabins are of rugged log construction.

can-eat bar of greens and garnishes. For those inclined to gamble for a meal, fishing is right outside the cabin door—by license in the Pecos or from the inn's three well-stocked ponds. Clean your catch, and the kitchen will cook it at any meal.

The Pecos Wilderness is a trail rider's or hiker's dream; the ranch offers guided trips for nature lovers and hunters, and riding lessons are available for novices. A superior winter retreat, Tres Lagunas is a haven for cross-country skiing, ice fishing, and ice skating. A cheering thermos of hot buttered rum is the perfect complement to a traditional sleigh ride.

In addition to the great outdoors, guests can plan to enjoy Santa Fe as well. It's just a forty-five-minute ride from Pecos Wilderness to the opera!

Left: Ponderosa pines shade the main lodge. OVERLEAF: The Pecos River runs through the ranch, providing the horses with much-needed water.

TRES LAGUNAS GUEST RANCH, Rt. 2, Box 100, Pecos, N. Mex. 87552; (505) 757-6194; Tom Walker, Innkeeper. Rustic main lodge of five guest rooms, four duplex cabins, three family cabins, and two bunkhouses with three rooms each; some fireplaces; private and shared baths. Open year round. Rates, including three delicious meals per day, from $47 per person double occupancy in lodge, to $60 each double in deluxe cabin. Buffet-style breakfast and lunch; dinner entree varies nightly, with Mexican dinner and outdoor steak barbecue being especially fine. Trout caught by guest will be cooked for any meal. Children welcome; pets by special arrangement. MasterCard and Visa credit cards accepted. An exhilarating, outdoors-oriented ranch for the aficionado and the novice alike; excellent fishing, hunting trips (elk, deer, mountain lion, grouse); riding lessons, swimming pool; sleigh rides and cross-country skiing.

DIRECTIONS: From Albuquerque, take I-25 north to exit 299 (Glorietta/Pecos). Turn left over freeway, then right into Pecos. Left at Pecos onto Rte. 63, then 12 miles to ranch. From Denver, take I-25 south past Las Vegas to the Rowe exit, Rte. 63. Right on 63 into Pecos. 12 miles to ranch.

BEAR MOUNTAIN RANCH

Silver City   **NEW MEXICO**

An innkeeper who loves nature

Straddling the magnificent Continental Divide, Bear Mountain is a haven for bird and beast. Nestled snugly amid aromatic piñon pine and juniper, the Bear Mountain Guest Ranch, guided by the sensitive hand of innkeeper Myra McCormick, melds into its setting and enhances nature's delicate balance.

The driving interests here are bird-watching and botanizing; die-hards and novices alike call it seventh heaven. Enter the sprawling stucco hacienda and discover a spacious, rustic study, flanked by massive stone fireplaces and stocked with books and botanical specimens both rare and common. Pass through to the solarium/dining room, where the central table is strewn with books and binoculars; hummingbird feeders attached to the windows offer rosy sweet nectar to these fleeting, jewel-like sprites. Around the yards, flat-topped bird feeders, with their constant supply of milo and sunflower seeds, and several watering spots attract flocks of birds—and jackrabbits. Few inns can boast Bear Mountain's colorful variety of guests.

"What astonishes most people, including experienced birdwatchers," says Myra, "is that out of the 743 species of birds in the United States, 422 are found in New Mexico."

A seemingly inexhaustible source of enthusiasm and energy, Myra is also the ranch's chief cook and displays a formidable talent for bread baking. Each meal is toothsome and thoughtfully prepared—Myra is as adamant about wholesome food as she is about conservation, current affairs, and New Mexican flora and fauna. Spirited discussions that begin over her family style dinners usually carry on into the night; that is, until one and all are lulled into silence by the flicker of a comforting fire.

Practicality and the stewardship of natural resources are the bedrock upon which this ranch is founded. Thus accommodations, which include spacious suites and fully equipped cottages, are simple and comfortable.

A born philosopher and teacher, Myra offers insight into her fascination with and love for nature. "There are some things we human beings take joy in that have nothing to do with making money or getting ahead. And when you get interested in something

Left: Innkeeper Myra McCormick and Tawny.

The sunlit interior of the hacienda.

outside of yourself you become an interesting person." Myra McCormick is living proof of this philosophy.

BEAR MOUNTAIN GUEST RANCH, P.O. Box 1163, Silver City, N. Mex. 88061; (505) 538-2538; Myra B. McCormick, Innkeeper. A large Spanish hacienda, two guest houses, and a small cottage, comprising twelve guest rooms with private baths, tub or shower. Open year round. Restaurant serves three meals, including family-style dinner; sack lunches packed for hikers and picnickers. Guests may bring liquor. Rates from $24.60 double in small house with kitchen, to $52.30 double in hacienda, the latter including meals; weekly rates available. Children welcome; well-behaved pets permitted. No credit cards accepted; personal check accepted if advance deposit has been received. Wilderness lodge offers unparalleled birdwatching, wild plant identification, mountain scenery; ghost towns and Indian ruins nearby.

DIRECTIONS: From Albuquerque, take I-25 south to NM Rte. 90. Take 90 (later 90/180) into Silver City. Stay on 180 (avoiding business district 180) to Alabama St. Turn right and go 2.8 miles to first cattle guard. Past guard turn left onto dirt road marked with dead end sign—this is Bear Mountain Ranch. House is .6 mile down drive. From Tucson, I-10 east to Lordsburg. Right at old-fashioned cloverleaf marked NM 90. See directions above.

PRIDE HOUSE

Jefferson   **TEXAS**

As pretty as a wedding cake

"An old house tells you what to do. I listened to what the house said." Pride House clearly communicated to Sandy Spalding that it wanted to be beautiful.

Sandy and her husband Ray discovered Jefferson on a Sunday drive in 1976. Inveterate restorers, they felt immediately at home in its unique antebellum and Victorian ambience; their move there was only a matter of time. To become a part of the working community they opened a restaurant, in partnership with Sandy's mother, Ruthmary, whose prowess in the kitchen is formidable and renowned. All the while they had their eye on the 'gingerbread house,' an ornate Victorian structure suffering from neglect and fire damage, and an accompanying old-fashioned guest house. When the owners offered the property for sale the Spaldings snapped it up. "To make it pay we decided to open a bed-and-breakfast. I had never been to one before. In fact, I didn't really know what a bed-and-breakfast was," Sandy confides with a laugh.

However naively this project may have started, no hint of inexperience or uncertainty remains. The Spaldings worked feverishly to give their inn the atmosphere they envisioned, and the result is a house as pretty as a wedding cake. They painted the clapboard exterior a rich *café au lait,* and laced its trim in white and baby blue. The front porch is filled with rockers, a swing, and cool, green ferns. Bedrooms are identified by color; the Green Room, for example, has deep forest green walls, a red and white country spread covering an iron and brass bed, and a fireplace shielded by a red-lacquer-and-bronze grate. The Blue Room, with soft blue walls, affords a king-size bed dressed with a mattress ticking spread and lace-edged dust ruffle, a table-for-two with comfortable chairs, and shutters lined with fabric.

Currently, Pride House is being managed by Ruthmary while Ray and Sandy and son Pride, after whom the inn is named, are off to the Northwest to mine gold. Ruthmary serves a large breakfast, stocks goodies in the kitchen for midnight snacks, and will cook up a dinner upon special request. Her culinary repertoire, which she characterizes as "folksy gourmet with a Cajun influence," includes jambalaya, shrimp creole, and crawfish *étouffée.*

The front parlor.

Before embarking on her Northwest adventure, Sandy summed up the real beauty of innkeeping. "An inn is a marvelous way to restore a historic place, share it with people, and make it pay its way. It's a very special thing."

PRIDE HOUSE, 409 Broadway, Jefferson, Tex. 75657; (214) 665-2675; Ruthmary Jordan, Innkeeper. Delightful Victorian frame house dating to 1889, with dependency house of same vintage. Open year round. Five guest rooms in house, each having private bath with tub or shower; country-style guest house sleeps six, with shared shower and tub. Rates, including continental breakfast, $40; $5 for each additional occupant. The inn serves breakfast seven days per week, country Creole dinner by special request. Guests may bring liquor. Well-behaved children and pets welcome in some facilities. No credit cards, but checks are accepted. Area offers fishing and water sports; house tours; antique shopping.

DIRECTIONS: From Dallas, take I-20 east to US 59 (Marshall exit); go north twenty miles to Jefferson; turn right in midtown onto Rte. 49; east to Pride House. From Shreveport, take I-20 west to US 59-Marshall; see directions above.

A prize restoration

In its day, the Excelsior was one of the premier hotels in the Southwest, made of brick and mortar, with a lacy, ironwork gallery in the front to give it a touch of Louisiana. In fact, in the nineteenth century, the Excelsior was the site of the Queen Mab balls, which were part of their own Mardi Gras celebration, with parades and floats that rivaled anything in New Orleans at the time.

The Excelsior drew famous guests from all over the world. The Barrymores always took a suite here when their touring company came to town. Oscar Wilde was enchanted by the formal patio garden in the back when he stopped here during his whirlwind lecture tour of America in 1882. The hotel was a great favorite with the members of the nineteenth-century American social aristocracy such as the Vanderbilts and the Whitneys. Presidents Ulysses S. Grant and Rutherford B. Hayes both entertained in the lavishly decorated ballroom.

In the late 1950s, the ladies of the Jesse Allen Wise Garden Club initiated a vigorous campaign to restore Jefferson to its glory days. Their prize restoration is the old Excelsior House. The club members swarmed over the hotel—scraping, sanding, refinishing, and reupholstering every piece of furniture in the place. Although mostly amateurs, in 1961 they received a special governor's citation for one of the finest restorations in the state.

All fourteen upstairs rooms are furnished with delightful museum-quality country antiques of maple, cherry, and mahogany. Lady Bird Johnson went to high school in Jefferson and has taken a special interest in the restoration of the Excelsior and in the rest of the community. The gold clock over the main fireplace is a gift from the former first lady.

Cissie McCampbell has been manager of the Excelsior for more than fifteen years and still supervises her famous plantation breakfasts in a sunny nook off the garden in back. Breakfast at the Excelsior, the

The parlor, with citations on the wall honoring the restoration.

only meal served except for special parties, is hearty Texas fare consisting of bacon, eggs, grits, freshly squeezed orange juice, and Cissie's own special bite-size Orange Blossom muffins, which literally melt in one's mouth.

The town of Jefferson is a delightful place for a quiet stroll and a relaxed historical tour. There is the Jefferson Museum to explore and the Carnegie Library, a fine old Classical Revival structure that contains one of the finest collections of old dolls in the state.

Left: The front desk, which was covered with many layers of paint before being restored to its natural finish. OVERLEAF: The magnificent canopied bed in the Presidential Suite, and the ballroom, with its pressed tin ceiling and Belter table.

EXCELSIOR HOUSE, 211 West Austin St., Jefferson, Tex. 75657; (214) 665-2513; Cissie McCampbell, Innkeeper. Gracious, elegant Victorian house in a river town remarkably well-preserved. Open year round. Double occupancy rates range from $25 to $35; two-bedroom suites available for $50. Private and shared baths. Full breakfast additional. No credit cards accepted.

DIRECTIONS: Jefferson is about 200 miles east of Dallas and 250 miles north of Houston. The inn is located off Polk Street, in the heart of Jefferson.

Granbury # THE NUTT HOUSE

An old-time Texas hotel delightfully restored

After the Civil War, Jesse and Jacob Nutt, two blind Missouri merchants, settled Granbury and operated the town mercantile; when their nephew, David Lee, was twelve he joined the business and became the brothers' eyes. Years passed. David took a wife, Sudie, and business boomed. With no hotel in the vicinity, David and Sudie began taking drummers and stagecoach passengers into their home, which became known as the "Nutt House," as was the limestone hotel they later built in the town.

After spending her adult life traveling the world with her military husband, Mary Lou Watkins returned to her hometown and decided to restore the hotel, although she now whispers confidentially: "If I had known what I was getting into I probably wouldn't have done it." Thank goodness for blissful ignorance, for today the Nutt House is a fine country hotel with a high culinary reputation.

Beyond a set of swinging screen doors, the dining room hearkens back to days of simpler living. Its walls abound with old maps of the town and framed needlepoint proverbs, and fresh flowers bedeck each table. Add to this a plate rail display of age-softened china, an early American cloth rug, a rugged stone fireplace, and the result is a restaurant whose charm is irresistible.

The menu is also reverent of the past. "We try to set our table as our mothers and grandmothers did at the turn of the century," explains Mary Lou. Meals are served buffet style, and a typical menu might include chicken and dumplings, homemade meatloaf, a selection of hot vegetables and cold salads, and three favorites of the house—hot water cornbread, a crispy, crunchy shell surrounding a tender heart; hot peach cobbler; and German buttermilk pie.

The guestrooms upstairs straddle long double hallways. Each has two doors, one hardwood and one screen, an old fashioned paddle fan, floral print curtains which arch in a graceful ruffle at the top of each slender window, and iron bedsteads. Customarily the earliest riser makes the morning's coffee in the pot at the end of the hall.

The crown jewel of Granbury's square is the old Opera House. Built in 1866, it stood empty and roofless for many years until its rescue in 1975. It now offers year-round performances of professional quality.

THE NUTT HOUSE HOTEL, Town Square, Granbury, Tex. 76048; (817) 573-5612; Mary Lou Watkins, Innkeeper. Simple, comfortable accommodations in historic mercantile building of hand-hewn local limestone. Open year round. Eight guest rooms sharing three baths with showers; one apartment with private bath. Rates $12.84 single; $21.40 double; apartment $32.10; $5.00 for each additional person. Reservations recommended. Dining room serves lunch seven days, supper Friday night. Liquor not permitted. No credit cards accepted. Children welcome; pets not allowed. Immediate vicinity offers excellent fishing and antique shopping; numerous sites of historical interest.

DIRECTIONS: From Waco, take I-35 north to Fort Worth, then Hwy. 377 south into Granbury.

Innkeeper Mary Lou Watkins.
Left: The lobby was once the town mercantile.

HEMPSTEAD INN

Unforgettable innkeepers and memorable food

Ghazi Issa was reared in Lebanon, the son of a wealthy family. But when he came to America to complete his education Ghazi studied the culinary arts. By opening an inn, he and wife Anne, who was an accountant in Houston, found a way to be on their own.

As one might expect, the Hempstead's raison d'etre is food. There is no written menu; the Issas offer the freshest market produce. The typical luncheon menu is extravagantly generous and features Southern cooking. Buttery pan fried chicken, beef brisket, meat loaf, chicken fried steak, a choice of at least ten vegetables and salads, and fresh-baked corn bread or biscuits are served family-style each day. At the evening meal, Ghazi plans to offer a selection of game meats—quail, partridge, duck, and pheasant—along with his Southern specialities.

After dining, the bit of exercise you'll most enjoy is a slow climb to the second floor guest rooms.

Though they'll win no prize for interior design, they are quite comfortable and offer the perfect place to digest Ghazi's cuisine.

HEMPSTEAD INN, 435 Tenth St. (Highway 290 N), Hempstead, Tex. 77445; (713) 826-6379; Anne and Ghazi Issa, Innkeepers. Victorian frame house built in 1901. Open year round. Eight guest rooms, four having private baths and four sharing one bath. Rates from $25 per room. Dining room serves lunch and dinner; homemade pastries for breakfast. Liquor permitted in room only. All major credit cards accepted. Children not encouraged; dogs on leashes permitted. Excellent bass and catfish fishing; Watermelon Capital of Texas; historic plantations; one hour to downtown Houston.

DIRECTIONS: From Houston, take Hwy. 290 north to Hempstead Inn. From Austin, 290 south to inn; From Waco, Hwy. 6 south (6 and 290 are the same at Hempstead).

Exterior grandeur, interior elegance

Although the Driskill today is a bit larger than the average country inn, it began as a visionary's dream back when Austin was no more than a dusty cow town—the westernmost town in Texas. The original building is a limestone landmark of Romanesque design, built in 1886 by cattle baron Colonel J. L. Driskill, who strongly believed in the future of the city.

The exterior grandeur and interior elegance of the Driskill, however incongruous they may have seemed in those early days, are perfectly suited to what is now the Lone Star State's cosmopolitan capital. The lobby is one of the handsomest in the region. Through the years the hotel was expanded to accommodate a burgeoning flow of traffic. The original building still offers rooms of old-fashioned comfort and gentility. VIP service makes a stay on one of the upper four floors of the newest wing an unforgettable experience. Guests in these rose-and-green quarters are greeted upon arrival by a bowl of fresh fruit and a bottle of wine; each morning a complimentary *Wall Street Journal* or local paper and a pot of coffee await your call. And although the hotel's gracious concierge, Catherine Weir, is available for all guests, she gives her special attention to the needs of guests on these four floors.

THE DRISKILL, 117 E. Seventh St., Austin, Tex. 78701; (512) 474-5911, toll-free 1-800-252-9367; Morgan Burkett, General Manager; Catherine Weir, Concierge. Elegant city hotel; Romanesque limestone facade painted grey; grand lobby. Open all year. Three meals per day year round in Dining Room; Bar and Grill closed Sundays. 180 guest rooms, one penthouse, and several suites; all rooms have bath with tub or shower. Rates $33 to $74 single; $42 to $84 double; suites up to $475 for penthouse. Children under 18 free. Children and pets welcome. All major credit cards are accepted. University of Texas campus nearby. Barton Springs, a natural spring surrounded by park, offers swimming and picnicking. Excellent dining and shopping in downtown Austin.

DIRECTIONS: From San Antonio, take I-35 north to 6th Street-12th Street exit. Take 6th Street west to Congress. Turn right to 7th. Turn right on 7th to hotel. Valet parking service in front of hotel. From Dallas, take I-35 south to exit marked 8th-3rd. Turn right on 6th. Turn right onto Congress, then onto 7th, and right again to hotel.

OVERLEAF: The Driskill's new lobby.

Princely pleasures of vintage Victorian

When Texas takes to counting her charms, the Prince Solms Inn should be high on the list. Its modest tan brick facade belies the splendors of a vintage Victorian interior. Guests enter through an enclosed, brick-paved garden, where an authentic *fachwerk* house, predating the inn, stands in European quaintness. The main hallway is resplendent with classic black-and-white tile flooring, a dramatic fireplace, its mantle bedecked with lustrous silk flowers and crowned with an ornate gilt mirror, and striking period wallpaper—full-blown pink and white roses on a background of gray lattice. It is here that innkeeper Larry Koehler offers the official welcome. Larry is infectiously proud of the Prince Solms and will gladly give a tour, starting with a bit of history.

In 1898 Emilie Eggeling, proprietor of New Braunfels's popular Plaza Hotel, decided to provide herself

Left: The hall mirror reflects an adjoining parlor.

with some competition. Hiring German designer Christian Herry, she set about building "the best looking little inn in the entire countryside." Herry ensured the sturdy structure a light and pleasant interior by installing a giant skylight in the center of the roof. When the hotel opened, its fame quickly spread; guests arriving by train from San Antonio and Austin were picked up at the station in a fringe-topped surrey.

When the Eggeling family sold the inn in the 1950s, the new owners began extensive remodeling, including the installation of an unobtrusive central air conditioning system and old-fashioned paddle fans in every room. Each of the eight upstairs guest rooms has been christened according to its unique decor. The wallpaper of the Magnolia guest room, for example, features bands of the bold blossom on a soft green field. A brass-and-iron double bed and celery green swag curtains complement the cool and sumptuous mood. Library, another guest room, as

The bar in Wolfgang's Keller.

in these suites to the aroma of breakfast on an English teacart just outside the door.

Dining at the Prince Solms is a princely pleasure; specialties of the house include a heavenly rendition of chicken breast *picata*, or the same served *à la provençale*. Like a Manhattan bistro transplanted to the Lone Star State, Wolfgang's Keller offers fine food and lively conversation to the tune of classics from a grand piano that serves as the room's centerpiece.

might be expected offers shelves of books; the king-size bed and a pair of easy chairs are perfect spots for curling up with a classic Western set in the region. A central hallway envelops the main staircase in ruby red. In one corner stands an antique sideboard, repository for the fragrant coffee and pastries each morning, as well as an ever-present bowl of fresh fruit. The two spacious downstairs suites include tiny kitchenettes and full-size living rooms; rise and shine

Right: Victorian blossoms enrich a first floor suite.
OVERLEAF: The Prince Solms at dusk.

THE PRINCE SOLMS INN, 295 E. San Antonio St., New Braunfels, Tex. 78130; (512) 625-9169; Larry Koehler, Innkeeper. Victorian style hotel with distinctive German influence typical of the region. Open year round. Eight guest rooms and two suites, all having baths with tub or shower. Rates, including continental breakfast, $35 to $45 single; $42 to $60 double; suite $75 to $85 double; $85 to $95 for three or more. Restaurant serves dinner Tuesday through Sunday. No children under sixteen; no pets allowed. MasterCard and Visa credit cards accepted. Area offers good fising; canoeing, tubing, and rafting on local rivers; tennis ranch nearby; spectacular caves.

DIRECTIONS: From San Antonio, take IH 35 north to Lake McQueeney exit; go left under underpass to town plaza; hotel is one block to right of plaza. From Austin, take IH 35 south to Lake McQueeney exit and turn right into town.

Second floor guest rooms open onto the skylighted staircase.

In New Braunfels— an uncommon Texas town

From the appearance of its exterior, the Faust Hotel might be any respectable old commercial building in any small American town, its blockish form enlivened with the requisite stone relief carving and the grace note of a small fountain. But here ends the Faust's flirtation with the typical. The lobby is a gem of hospitable elegance. Rich oriental carpets dress the glistening tile floor. Brocade and velvet antique chairs and sofas abound. The original registration desk and ornate cash register, a grandfather clock, large potted trees, and ceiling fans restore a bygone nuance to the word *hotel.*

While the dining room and bar are less successfully refurbished, with a heavy emphasis on "Tropical garden" ambience, the food is quite presentable.

Built in 1928, the four-story structure was known successively as the Traveller's Hotel, the Hotel Faust (after one of its founders), and most recently, the Honeymoon Hotel; vintage photographs of nervous newlyweds decorate the dining room walls. Rescued from oblivion by an enterprising businessman, the Faust offers bright, clean, and comfortable guest rooms; most are furnished with original beds and dressers, refinished in a warm glow.

New Braunfels affords a plethora of activities for visitors of all ages. The famous Wurstfest is an annual autumn extravaganza. The Comal County Fair, a wealth of antique shops, tubing on the sparkling Comal River, and wild whitewater rafting on the Gaudelupe make for a memorable stay.

FAUST HOTEL, 240 S. Seguin St., New Braunfels, Tex. 78130; (512) 625-7791; Patti Thompson, Innkeeper. Vintage small-town hotel offering sixty-two guest rooms and one suite, each with private bath. Open year round. Rates $30 to $45, varying according to room size and occupancy. Veranda Restaurant serves three meals per day six days, breakfast and lunch on Sundays. Visa, MasterCard, American Express, and Carte Blanche credit cards accepted. Children welcome; pets not allowed. Water sports on nearby lake and rivers; plentiful antique shopping.

DIRECTIONS: From San Antonio take I-35 north to McQueeney exit. Turn left under underpass into New Braunfels on Seguin St. Hotel is one block before town plaza. From Auston, take I-35 south to McQueeney exit and bear right into town. See directions above.

The charmingly restored lobby of a small hotel.

HOTEL ST. ANTHONY

San Antonio   **TEXAS**

Classic grandeur in the land of dust and sage

"The Waldorf of the Prairie," the St. Anthony, located in the city of its patron's Spanish name, is one of America's most gracious hostelries. The two Texas cattlemen who built it in 1909 spared no expense in importing Eastern elegance to the land of dust and sage. In 1936 Ralph Morrison purchased The St. Anthony as a pet project. A world traveler and collector of fine art, he filled the hotel with *objets* from around the globe, including a sumptuous, rose-wood-inlaid Steinway piano, James Ferdinand McCann's painting "Monarch of the Golden West", Chinese urns, splendid crystal chandeliers, a lovely collection of bronze, marble, and alabaster statuary, and much more, all of which remain today. Twice daily a string ensemble performed in front of the massive woodburning fireplace—a tradition soon to be resumed.

Morrison's was the first hotel in America to be completely air conditioned. He installed electric-eye doors for the convenience of patron and bellhop alike and instituted drive-in registration so that new arrivals would be spared trooping through the elegant lobby in rumpled traveling clothes.

The St. Anthony, which is being carefully returned to its original grandeur, is ideally located for shopping, sightseeing, and dining; the lobby, overlooking a shady park, is just two blocks from both the River Walk and the Alamo.

HOTEL ST. ANTHONY (INTERCONTINENTAL), 300 E. Travis, San Antonio, Tex. 78298; P.O. Box 2411; (512)-227-4392. W. Andrews Kirmse, General Manager; Richard J. Kinnally, front office manager. Elegant city hotel across from small park. Open year round. 398 guest rooms; all have bath and shower. Rates $50 to $68 single; $60 to $78 double; $84 to $110 triple; suites $137 to $360. Children under 12 free, if no additional beds are needed. No pets allowed. Two restaurants offer three meals per day year round, open to public. All major credit cards accepted. Roof-top swimming pool and tennis courts planned for 1983. Conveniently located in historic San Antonio, near River Walk and Alamo.

DIRECTIONS: From Austin, take I-35 south to Houston Street exit. Left on Houston to Jefferson (the back of the hotel is on your left). Left onto Travis, which has motor entrance. From Houston, take I-10 west to I-37. North to Commerce St. Left on Commerce to Presa (which becomes Jefferson), then right to hotel. Parking garage on Travis.

The opulent, treasure-filled lobby of a grand hotel.

San Antonio   # MENGER HOTEL   **TEXAS**

The elegant old west next door to the Alamo

William A. Menger was a German brewer who came to San Antonio and married Mrs. Mary Guenther, a young widow who operated a boarding house there. Under their combined efforts, what had been a modest establishment quickly outgrew its quarters. In 1855, just twenty-one years after the fall of the Alamo, the Mengers built a new boarding house on Alamo Plaza, next door to the famed mission. By 1857 they were ready to take on a more ambitious project—this time to build "the finest hotel west of the Mississippi."

Today the Menger proper occupies an entire city block. But the Spanish-style grillwork porch and balconies of the original building are as picturesque now as they were then. Inside the old wing, the classical three-story rotunda, supported by massive columns and capped with a stained glass skylight, seems to echo the whispers of a romantic past. The famous Menger bar, with solid cherry counter and ceiling modeled after the House of Lords' bar in London, is where Teddy Roosevelt recruited his Rough Riders. The patio, a tropical garden off the lobby, is said to contain the cottonwood trees for which the Alamo was named.

The twenty-five original guest rooms likewise cast a spell of history; all are furnished with original antiques, including full canopy beds and marble-topped dressers and nightstands. As a change of pace, the Roy Rogers Suite is appropriately outfitted in rawhide and burnished leather.

Left: The magnificent detailing and graceful proportions of the rotunda complement the wrought iron façade shown below.

THE MENGER HOTEL, 204 Alamo Plaza, San Antonio, Tex. 78205; (512) 223-4361; reservations 1-800-327-9157; Arthur L. Abbott, General Manager. Restored original Spanish-flavored structure with delicate grillwork and balconies overlooking street; modern additions. Open year round. Three hundred and twenty guest rooms, each with private bath and color television. Rates $33 to $45 single; $45 to $55 double. Coffee Shop serves breakfast and lunch, dining room three meals, seven days per week. Children and small pets welcome. All major credit cards accepted. Ideally situated in the heart of San Antonio, next door to the Alamo.

DIRECTIONS: From any direction, follow signs to Alamo— Menger is next door.

San Antonio's beautiful River Walk is a must for visitors.

LANDMARK INN

A stay at the Landmark is a stroll through history

The Alsatian motto "He who values his own tranquility knows to respect that of others" adorns each room at the Landmark Inn in Castroville, "The Little Alsace of Texas." An inn that holds to such a standard needs no higher recommendation, but its philosophy is just the beginning of the Landmark's historic charm.

Castroville was founded on September 3, 1844 by Henri Castro, an adventurous Frenchman who led 700 families from Alsace-Lorraine to the fledgling Texas republic. By 1849 Cesar Monod had built a sturdy, one-story, plastered limestone building on the banks of the Medina River, and had opened a general store in his home. In 1853 John Vance, an Irish immigrant, bought the property, added a second story, built a two-story bathhouse—the only one between San Antonio and the border—constructed another home for himself next door, and opened a hotel for travelers.

By 1854 the area was Castroville's industrial center: a gristmill, dam, and cotton gin were constructed on Vance's property and these prospered grandly for sixty years until management changed and business deteriorated. In 1925, and just in the nick of time, New Orleans businessman Jordan Lawler purchased, repaired, and improved the property, bringing Castroville its first waterworks and electric power plant; meanwhile sister Ruth took over the guesthouse and renamed it Landmark Inn to commemorate the important role it had played in the history of Castroville. Miss Lawler operated a genteel inn until 1974 when she retired and donated the entire property to the Texas Parks and Wildlife Service. Today, Ruth Lawler lives in the house that John Vance built, and guests stay in the original inn and converted bathhouse.

Restoration of the hostel has been painstaking—and a bit unorthodox. In addition to preserving the unique Alsatian character of the architecture, with its stark plaster walls, forest green doors, and red tin roofs, restorers have sought also to capture the flavor of the thriving inn as Miss Lawler operated it in the 1940s. Thus each room is a homey mix of period styles. Care was taken to paint interiors in colors popular during the forties; to reproduce the original linoleum, restorers tracked down a Dutch firm that still makes the old-fashioned floor covering.

A stay at the Landmark is a stroll through history—from the artful industriousness of homesick pioneers to the simple pleasures of a more recent past.

LANDMARK INN, P.O. Box 577, Castroville, Tex. 78009; (512) 538-2133; Carolyn Scheffer, Manager. Picturesque Alsatian farmhouse and outbuildings of white plastered limestone with red tin roofs; restored interiors reflect the compound's heyday as an inn in the 1940s. Open year round. Eight guest rooms, one equipped for handicapped; two rooms in converted bathhouse; some private baths, some shared. Rates $13 single; $16 double; $1 for children six through twelve. No dining facilities at inn. Liquor permitted in rooms only. Children welcome; no pets allowed. No credit cards, but checks are accepted. Fascinating area scenically and historically; good river fishing; beautifully restored town built by Alsatian immigrants.
DIRECTIONS: From San Antonio, take US90 west directly to Landmark Inn. One block before Medina River bridge.

Left: Glorious fields of hybrid sunflowers around Castroville have a practical use—the seeds make excellent fuel oil.

THE
LICKSKILLET
INN

There is no Room at the Inn!

Information

LICKSKILLET INN

Fayetteville

The way of life today of generations past

Jeanette Donaldson's dream house, yellow frame with a white picket fence and two porch swings, is a far cry from the home she and husband Steve shared in Houston. Determined to escape the urban pressure-cooker, the Donaldsons made Fayetteville their home, and their home the Lickskillet Inn.

Believed to be the oldest house in a town once called Lickskillet, the original structure, built around 1853, sported an open "dog run" flanked by four rooms. Now enclosed, these guest rooms are named after Fayetteville's forefathers: Cummings, Ross, Crier, Shaver—all but the last members of Stephen Austin's "original 300 settlers." Each room has its own wood burning stove and is decorated with a charming collection of antiques and bric-a-brac reflecting Jeanette's warmhearted spirit. During the evening the inn converts to kerosene light which casts

Left: The good old days in Smalltown, U.S.A. are alive and well at this fine inn.

a soft romantic glow. According to the Donaldsons, most people enjoy waking in the middle of a winter's night to stoke the fire. Not only is it cozy but it's also a great way to appreciate life in generations past.

THE LICKSKILLET INN, P.O Box 85, Fayetteville, Tex. 78940; (713) 378-2846; Steve and Jeanette Donaldson, Innkeepers. Oldest house in Fayetteville; cottage built 1853, Victorian embellishments added 1875. Open year round. Four guest rooms, sharing one bath with shower attachment. Rates, including continental breakfast, $30 single; $30 to $40 double; $5 for extra bed. Air conditioning available in all rooms. No restaurant or bar, but guests may bring liquor. Children not encouraged; pets not allowed. MasterCard, American Express, Visa credit cards accepted. Nearby Lake Fayetteville, a 2400-acre "Trophy Bass Lake" (no catch measuring less than 16" may be kept); plentiful antique shopping in area; Festival Hill fourteen miles away in Round Top, Tex.

DIRECTIONS: From Houston, take I-10 west to Columbus. Turn right on second Columbus exit (Highway 71 to La Grange and Austin) and stay on Hwy. 71 approximately seventeen miles to Hwy. 955. Turn right, then proceed five miles to Fayetteville. In town, turn right onto Hwy. 159 (Main Street), then left at Fayette St. The Lickskillet is just beyond the square. From Austin, take Hwy. 71 for approximately 1½ hours out of Austin to Hwy. 955. See Houston directions above.

Jeanette's dream house.

Fayetteville # THE COUNTRY PLACE **TEXAS**

The comforts of smalltown life

Unlike most urbanites who flee the city, Clovis and Maryann Heimsath left Houston in search of the future. Clovis, a successful architect and painter, and Maryann, an artist as well as business partner, explored Texas in preparation for a book about the state's historic buildings. When their project took them to Fayetteville, a town of some four hundred souls, it was love at first sight, and they headed for the drawing board.

After several foiled attempts at combined living and working in their adopted community, the Heimsath's hit upon a plan. They bought the Zapp commercial building, which was built on the town square in 1900, and transplanted Clovis's central architectural office to its main floor; a branch office was kept open in Houston. When they began renting the second-floor rooms country inn-style and started a restaurant in the rear, The Country Place was an immediate hit.

This is a charming and unselfconsciously authentic country hotel. Rough, whitewashed plank walls provide a rustic background for the melange of homey antiques. Large screened windows, a veranda with rocking chairs, ceiling fans that "condition" the air, and two shared bathrooms round out the old-fashioned feeling. Throughout, Maryann and Clovis's prints and paintings add sophistication.

The only locks to be found in The Country Place are a hook-and-eye on the door of each room. Often as not, guests arriving midweek are greeted with a handwritten note directing them to their quarters.

On weekdays, diners are introduced to the local array of Czech or German restaurants—this part of Texas is a cradle of Central European culture—but on weekends, dinner and a Sunday brunch make The Country Place the hamlet's culinary center. Operated by Carol and Perry Thacker, themselves transplanted Houstonians, the restaurant seats less than forty. A mix-and-match casualness prevails in the décor; antique tables, each dressed with fresh white cloth and wildflowers, are illuminated by simple hanging basket lamps.

Left: Innkeepers Maryann and Clovis Heimsath.

Each evening a single menu is offered. One night may feature a California-style Mexican repast, and the next a continental or American classic. The Black Forest pork chops and special Country Place chicken are sublime. Other highlights include chilled, creamed vegetable soups, subtly seasoned vegetables, and hot peach cobbler with whipped cream. Brunch brings a Texas-sized parade of courses, with the Fayetteville specialty, buttery, fruit-filled kolacky, featured front and center.

The Heimsaths see their delightful country inn more as a harbinger of the future than a reminder of the past. Clovis firmly believes that old buildings and the comforts of small-town life will be rediscovered by progressive architects and adopted as a sensible alternative to increasing complexity. Large windows that open, breezeways, shade trees, paddle fans, and high ceilings—they are the wave of the future, as Clovis sees it. Yesterday and tomorrow merge beautifully at The Country Place.

THE COUNTRY PLACE, On the Square, Box 39, Fayetteville, Tex. 78940; (713) 378-2712; Maryann and Clovis Heimsath, Innkeepers. Red brick turn-of-the-century commercial style building with balcony porches front and back; delightful period decor. Open year round. Eight guest rooms sharing two bathrooms, one with shower, one with tub. Restaurant serves country style dinner Friday and Saturday, popular Sunday brunch. Rates $15 per room. Children welcome. No credit cards, but checks accepted. Heart of Texas wildflower country; good fishing and antique shopping in area; Festival Hill Music festival nearby.

DIRECTIONS: From Houston, take I-10 west to Columbus. Turn right on second Columbus exit (Hwy 71 to La Grange and Austin) and stay on 71 approximately 17 miles to 955. Turn right, then proceed five miles to Fayetteville. The Country Place is on corner of town square. From Austin, take 71 for approximately 1½ hours out of town to Hwy. 955. See Houston directions above.

Eagle Lake # THE FARRIS 1912 **TEXAS**

Sophisticatedly homey; dramatically cozy

If inns had gender, the Farris 1912 would be a lady. A delicate wrought iron fence surrounds the pink brick building. Over the porch, paned double doors framed by a Palladian window open onto a small balcony. Inside, sumptuous colors evoke an intriguing spectrum of moods.

The tastes, talents, and teamwork of Helyn and Bill Farris created this delightful inn. When they purchased the premises at the close of 1974, it was a two-dollar-per-night flophouse, and much the worse for wear. "People thought we'd lost our minds when we took it on," laughs Bill. But the Farrises knew better. Active restorers for many years, they began fancying renovation of the hotel when Helyn's flower/antique shop outgrew its quarters. Since Bill was eligible for retirement at the time the building came up for sale, the purchase and the project seemed meant to be.

Salvaging much of its original charm—it was built as a luxury hotel in 1912—they did all of the refurbishing themselves, from cleaning, wiring, and plastering to painting and decorating. When it comes to the latter, Helyn's sensibilities are straight out of a classic interior design magazine, but her instincts demand comfort and warmth; the resultant blend at the Farris might be described as "sophisticatedly homey" or "dramatically cozy." The downstairs lobby and dining room are a luminous shade of new-leaf green; skylights enhance the fresh atmosphere with a shower of sunshine. In the two sitting rooms —one in deep red, the other pink—an old-fashioned rose pattern carpet provides a vivid complement to the color scheme and a rich background for a trove of antiques. Every room at the Farris is stocked with turn-of-the-century furnishings—and, as the hotel houses Helyn's flower and antique shop, most are for sale.

Upstairs, all bedrooms open into a large central lounge. Each bedroom carries out a color theme—butterscotch, melon, sky blue, purple, red—with Helyn's characteristic panache. Antique beds, chests, and wardrobes, including some rare Texas pieces, furnish each room. Though not all rooms have a private bath, the shared accommodations are pleasant and convenient.

Eagle Lake is known in sporting circles as the "Goose Hunting Capital of the World". Its surrounding rice fields serve as winter grounds for a staggering number of these fine feathered fowl. Naturally enough, from November through January, the Farris 1912 is a veritable hunter's haven. During this season, Bill and Helyn offer an American plan—all you can eat—room and board service. Hunters from all over the world converge on the inn year after year, its warm hospitality and mouthwatering fare a delightful contrast to the cold and damp of the marshes.

And so, like most ladies, the Farris has her moods; swinging from the pure and breathless creature of spring, standing at the gateway to the Texas wildflower country, to a *femme fatale* in autumn, attracting hardy huntsmen to her warm delights.

THE FARRIS 1912, 201 N. McCarty, Eagle Lake, Tex. 77434; (713) 234-2546; Helyn and Bill Farris, Innkeepers. Handsome reddish brick structure with Creole detailing of delicate green woodwork; comfortable vintage interiors. Closed Christmas Day. Sixteen guest rooms in main building, four two-bedroom suites in guest house; private and shared baths. Rates, including continental breakfast, $36 single; $48 double. Daily American meal plan offered during goose-hunting season (Nov. through Jan.); other months, dinner served Friday and Saturday. Beer and wine available, guests may bring liquor. No children under twelve; no pets allowed. All major credit cards accepted. Excellent waterfowl hunting and freshwater fishing in immediate area; birdwatching at national refuge; golf and tennis near hotel.

DIRECTIONS: From Houston, take either Hwy. FM 1093, 90A, or I-10 west to Eagle Lake. Hotel is on N.W. corner of town square. From San Antonio, take I-10 east to Eagle Lake exit.

Left: All guest rooms open onto a light-filled central lounge.

Palacios # LUTHER HOTEL **TEXAS**

Peace and quiet on the gulf coast

"We love this place and feel we offer something a little different," said innkeeper Elsie Luther. She and husband Charles purchased the Luther Hotel back in the early forties and still wax enthusiastic about their oasis on the coast. With some families planning their twelfth visit in twelve years the Luthers must be doing something right.

Presiding over a spacious, well-manicured lawn that sweeps to Tres Palacios Bay, the hotel has a quiet, homey atmosphere. The winter season—from December through April—brings "snowbirds" from northern climes who settle in to wait for the spring thaw. During the steamy Texas summer, city dwellers and families escape to cool beach breezes. Fishing, hunting, and long walks are popular pastimes, but, as Elsie says, "If you want excitement, don't come here!"

Left: A perennial guest, Alto Lee, displays a fine brace of ducks.

Accommodations range from single hotel rooms and apartments with working kitchens, to a private penthouse which is a favorite with newlyweds.

THE LUTHER HOTEL, South Bay Blvd., Palacios, Tex. 774;65; (512) 972-2312; Elsie and Charles Luther, Innkeepers. Weathered cypress structure with colonial-style pillars. Open year round. Seventeen hotel rooms, each with private bath; eleven motel units, three with living rooms and all having kitchens; twenty-four apartments; very private penthouse. Rates by room from $20 in hotel to $40 some apartments; penthouse $50. Recommended restaurant within two blocks. Children welcome; pets not permitted. Liquor permitted in rooms and game room. No credit cards, but travelers' cheques and personal checks accepted. Quiet, relaxed atmosphere; excellent fishing (trout, redfish, flounder) and crabbing; boat rentals; long bay frontage.

DIRECTIONS: From Houston, take U.S. 59 to Rte. 71 Palacios exit; turn left to Hwy. 35; well marked into town; left at first full traffic light. From Corpus Christi, take Hwy. 35 to Palacios; right at first full light.

BADLANDS HOTEL

Lajitas TEXAS

An air conditioned re-creation of the past

"When the Great Creator finished making the earth and the plants and the animals, He discovered He had a great pile of materials left over. He threw these into a heap and made the badlands of the Big Bend." Country inns are generally to be found in places of peace and refinement, and as this ancient Indian legend makes clear, the Big Bend area is not one of them. But that is what makes the Badlands Hotel so entrancing. In the midst of savage wilderness resides a perfectly comfortable, movie-set Western hotel complex, complete with tennis courts, swimming pool, restored adobe chapel, 4700-foot private landing strip, artist-in-residence workshop and gallery, and saloon—to name just a portion of what is going on in this wilderness resort.

The history of the area is as wild as its terrain; from Commanche and Apache raids, cattle and gold smuggling, the Mexican Revolution under Pancho Villa, and the nefarious dealings of assorted outlaws, bandits, and desperados, there has seldom been a quiet moment on this ford of the Rio Grande.

BADLANDS HOTEL, P.O. Box 18, Terlingua, Tex. 79852; (915) 371-2471; Tom and Emily Moore, Innkeepers. 'Movie-set' Western style hotel in resort community. Open year round. Seventeen rooms in hotel, twenty in reconstructed cavalry post, fifteen condominiums, three cabins; private and shared baths. Rates range from $35 double in cavalry post to $115 for three-bedroom house. Restaurant open seven days per week. Children and pets welcome. MasterCard, Visa, and American Express credit cards accepted. Plentiful recreation on premises, including swimming pool, tennis courts, horseback riding, river rafting, chuckwagon cookouts; 4700-ft. hard surface airstrip at inn.

DIRECTIONS: From Alpine, take Rte. 118 south to Study Butte; take 170 to Lajitas. From Presidio, take 170 southeast to Lajitas. By air: 155° radial from Marfa VOR—approx. 70 nautical miles.

Left: Big Bend country: the muddy Rio Grande reflects the spectacular cliffs on the Mexican side of the river.

The swimming pool, with the hotel complex in the background.

Fort Davis # INDIAN LODGE **TEXAS**

An adobe legacy of the Great Depression

Indian Lodge, a solitary, white adobe complex, commands the head of Keesey Canyon in the Davis Mountains, striking a vivid contrast to the surrounding terrain. The native vegetation—a borderland blend of desert yucca, agave, and cactus on the one hand and range grass, juniper, and oak on the other—gives a feeling of remoteness, the imagery of an outpost at the desert's edge.

The lodge was built by "the CCC boys" in 1933, and in keeping with that operation's philosophy it was built to last. The Civilian Conservation Corps gave jobs to hungry men; with nothing but time on their hands, they made their own adobe, built and carved the sturdy, New Mexican-style furniture, and trucked in reeds for the ceilings from the Rio Grande riverbed. Thoughtful planning allowed every room

Left: A west Texas sky over Fort Davis. OVERLEAF: Fort Davis, the historic military post made famous in many Western movies.

its own terrace entrance and mountain views on two or three sides. Because the lodge walls are a formidable twenty-eight inches thick and those of the rooms eighteen, Indian Lodge stays cool in the summer and retains warmth in the winter.

INDIAN LODGE, P.O. Box 786, Fort Davis, Tex. 79734; (915) 426-3254; Harvey Rhea, Manager; Jane Russell, Assistant Manager. Beautifully crafted pueblo-style inn built by Civilian Conservation Corps in 1933. Closed middle two weeks of January. Thirty-nine guest rooms, each with shower and tub. Restaurant offers three meals every day; simple, well-prepared American fare with some Mexican specialties; restaurant closed Christmas Day. Liquor permitted in rooms only. Rates $16.48 single; $18.54 to $21.63 double; $3 each additional occupant over 12 years of age; $1 children 6 to 12; no charge under 6. Pets not permitted. No credit cards, but travelers' cheques accepted. Swimming pool and children's playground on premises. McDonald Observatory and classic rugged Southwest scenery nearby.

DIRECTIONS: From El Paso, take I-10 east to 90 (Van Horn) and turn right. Left onto FM 505. Right at 166/118 into Fort Davis. Indian Lodge is in park four miles beyond town. From Midland, take I-20 west to Pecos. Get off freeway and go left on Rt. 17 into Balmorhea and beyond to Loop 118/166. Right on 166, three miles to park entrance.

Fort Davis SUTLER'S LIMPIA HOTEL

TEXAS

Restored with faithful accuracy

Fort Davis is a sun-drenched West Texas town, naturally cooled by the Davis Mountains. No street signs guide the way of the stranger, and much of the residential area is brushy pasture. At the center of town, next to the tree-shrouded courthouse, stands Sutler's Limpia Hotel, with its Boarding House Restaurant and Sutler's Store, a sizeable gift and plant shop. Built in 1912 to accommodate heat-stricken East Texans, the hotel is a sturdy edifice of pink limestone pieced like a jigsaw puzzle.

"The hotel is a work of love," proprietor J. C. Duncan reports, forthrightly proud. He and wife Isabelle have restored the Limpia with faithful accuracy, retaining its original turn-of-the-century character and adding a few latter-day amenities, such as concealed air conditioning and a glass-capped veranda. The Boarding House Restaurant features country specialties; regular offerings include southern fried or smothered chicken, chicken fried steak, grilled ham steak, and a special dessert each day, such as buttermilk pie.

Incidentally, there was no illustrious Sutler family in the Sutler Limpia's past. In these parts, 'sutlers' were civilians granted the right to supply soldiers with "clothing, groceries, and necessities" unavailable at the post—in this case the Fort Davis Military Post a mile down the road.

SUTLER'S LIMPIA HOTEL, P.O. Box 822, Fort Davis, Tex. 79734; (915) 426-3237. Isabelle and J. C. Duncan, Innkeepers. Charming country hotel built of pink limestone quarried at Fort Davis. Closed for three days at Christmas. Nine regular guest rooms, each with combination shower/tub; two suites, one with shower only. Rates, $25 to $32; $4 for each additional occupant. Children welcome; no pets allowed. Reservations are mandatory; no credit cards accepted. Restaurant, open to public, serves three meals Tuesday through Sunday. The county is dry, but all guests are automatic members of J. C.'s club, which serves liquor. Historic Fort Davis and McDonald Observatory are nearby.

DIRECTIONS: From El Paso, take I-10 east to 90 (Van Horn) and turn right. Left onto FM 505. Right at 166/118 into Fort Davis.

A real country hotel.